W0259779

HELLO SEROTONIN

HELLO SEROTONIN

JON PAUL FIORENTINO

COACH HOUSE BOOKS

www.jonpaulfiorentino.com

first edition, second printing

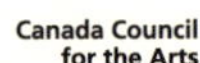

Published with the assistance of the Canada Council for the Arts and the Ontario Arts Council.
We acknowledge the financial support of the Government of Ontario through the Ontario Book Publishers Tax Credit program and the Government of Canada through the Book Publishing Industry Development Program (BPIDP).

NATIONAL LIBRARY OF CANADA CATALOGUING IN PUBLICATION

Fiorentino, Jon Paul
Hello serotonin / Jon Paul Fiorentino.

For Lilly

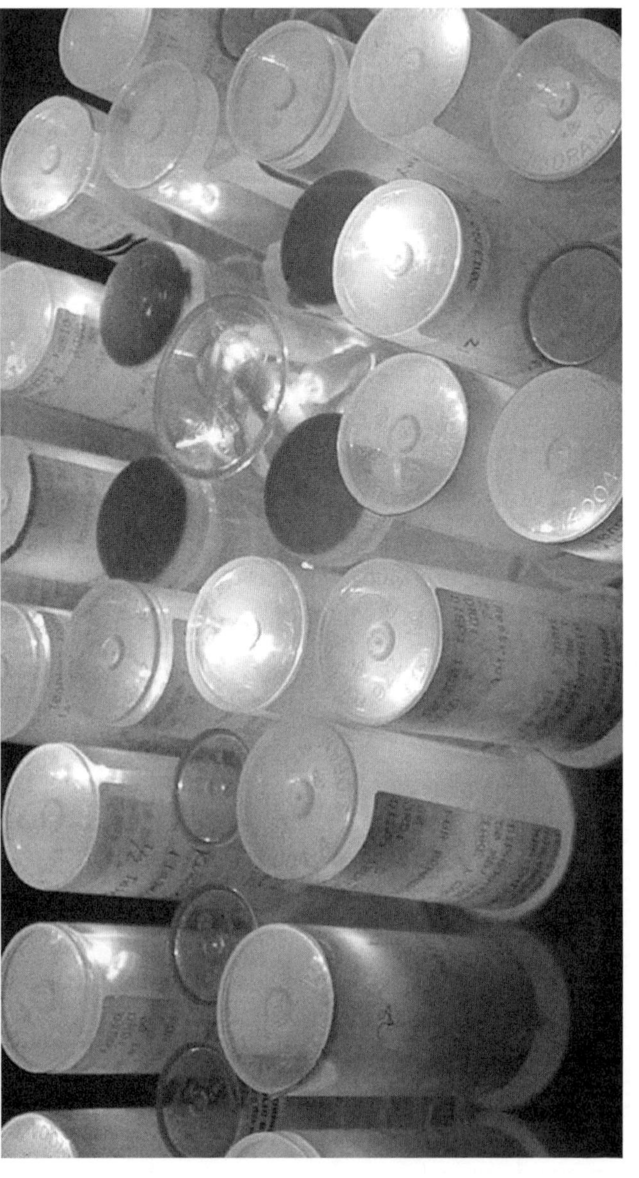

NEUROTRANSMISSIONS

NEUROTRANSMISSION

Another static dream tactic – don't call me home with
that tone; I get wistful when you don't call.

Remorse is a honey-tongued letter. *I'm traipsing along,* she
wrote; the bar glistened weakly behind her sheen.

When the phone rings my memory triggers, trips along;
a neurotransmission trips itself more real, filmic.

She whispers something and it sounds like someone
thrushed all night and a caffeine lullaby, valium dream.

Guilt umbrellas skyward from the trepanation stream –
kicked in the wit again.

Here is an abortive neurotransmission –
cold like an octave drop, relentless like the dial tone.

SERPENTINE RECEPTORS

Medusal adjectival restraint binds us.
I have a nanotechnological pen.
This neurotransmission has been cloned
from a worn-out textbook worm.

Across the transmembrane structures
after countless intracellular transfers
decentralization and desensitization
occur and infer something sinister:

inevitably, receptors refuse to listen.

ASTROCYTES

Astrocytes feed neurons
talk metatrophic trash to axon and dendrite
alike, depolarize the glucose fix.

Astrocytes deal from glial cells
spread neuronal love all over, all
around, dole out strophes.

Astrocytes need bliss
want the highs of recognition and transmission
but, starfucking is an acquired agency.

Astrocytes sing lullabies
signal the saddest dormancy
so, this time it's terminal.

PSYCHOMETRICS

can only dream in certain psychometrics
make-believe downpour circumvent grammar

eyes always make turn-away faces
hello pale grey pills absentee pronouns

roll calling naming missing
hymn stealing rhythm to come into

down whisper basement don't own
or give away psyche or order imperative

marginal taste fervour devour suggest
not firmament spread out like praxis

these eyes that flicker dream sublimate
can only watch metre like a paralytic

these eyes are yours they turn away like
passengers carrying on without you

I watch you inattentive come home
calling dream certain windows certain

pills certain minor chords certain rules
certain signs assigned and subverted

you
present

TAKEUP 1

take up reading a meandering dream lite

swallow on a neck pandering stress

powder feels underpaid plunderers

drip drips a blender rip-off

homing comes a coating of menthol

TAKEUP 2

reading
gaunt children hide in the neglected book stacks

sympathy
black-eyed susans wilt to the sound of a respirator

drivel
emotive sheet laced with inhalants, out of breath intoxic

coma
cigarettes expire on asphalt, trampled on by elders

powder
toxins spill on the dirty sidewalk home

TAKEUP 3

take up
the book

breathe in
a gasp of uptake

hello you
serotonin

take the
dream up

you have some nerve
you have some nerve

soma uptake
it's been a thrill

homing idiom
your body language

take up the drink
on the familial split jar

it's in your blood
it's in your blood

AGONISTICS

Strategic levels of agonists
Tangential levels of subjectivists

Stringent levels of athletics
Transient levels of subjunctivists

Malignant levels of constructs
Constrictive levels of triptychs

Metrical levels of clinicians
Cacophonous levels of treatments

DOPAMINE SONG

Dream.
Cut the tether
there.

Trill.
Let reverb last.
Plunge and purge.

Snap.
Let every neuron
fire and misfire.

Cut.
Underdress with a tourniquet.
Slam your way into sleep.

SOME THOUGHTS ON STRICT CONS

Hard to think of lightly
Precipitation tenors and their vehicles
Subtype infelicities (I thought so)
Thought to produce blissful thought
Felt as convulsive chemical release
Received as detox postcard

Hard to think of lately
Dopamine songs and their antecedents
Non-selective reciprocity (you, not you)
Dreamed of paracrine parasites
Woke up in Winnipeg
Revived with an excitatory blunt object

LET'S HEAR IT FOR HYDROXYTRYPTAMINE!

Hydroxytryptamine: why try in it.

Serotonergic agents inform the generic precursor.

Cholinergic neurons croon choleric, colicky.

Norepinephrine pens frenetic epics.

Parasympathomimesis is amiss, tragic, parallel.

Platonic agonists and antagonists wax nicotinic or not.

Dendritic desire misses the terminal button.

Meet me at the postsynaptic wrap party.

I'll be in the adrenalin room.

Hi!

HELLO SEROTONIN

HELLO SEROTONIN

the drip that fails to linger
sting that lures

where's the world at
speeding down the drain

paralinguist [read poet] scratching
at the window trope

let me intra prefix the mirror make
the cold night longer

held back hand-eye dreamer
reader meet alcohol

breathe desperate home touch
torch that tongue portal

hyperlure me home and find me
a section of hardwood

calm me down come down to
my level, level me

coming down like a system
needling into neurons

THRUSH HOUR

thrush hour:

pedestrian wake

suck out of bedthrust

taste last night

doors creak open

drones spill out

doors close and lock

on their own

spill onto streets on a retail kind of morning
exhaust on the tongue in the neurotranslation

. drip into office .
. every thrush needs tonic .
. hush into a commerce wake .
. everyone is cash-strapped .

TRASH

trash in the mind
trash of the world
man is half trash
all trash in the grave
– Allen Ginsberg

The elevator carries the trash
and the trash carry gilded cell phones.

The suits are hooked up for the weekend
and the revolution is stuck in voice mail.

The family has half a mind to stay
and the trash is on the corner six days early.

Buried in bungalows for the weekend and the television
carries on until the workweek.

Home is where the trash is; they are hooked there
elevated in their cells, cornered there, then
drawn back to work by a dirge ringtone – something like:
all trash in the grave . . .   and so on.

THE LOCUS EATERS

. not particularly happy
have you heard about the moment of locution .

. it might be our way out of speech
and into something else .

. competence and performance intersect
in a transient locus choral local .

. *fuck off* chime the melancholy choral locus eaters
I want to stay .

. performativity welcomes lexical preference
illocutions for the ill at heart .

. perlocutions all around it's on me
you know what I mean .

. the whole process latent as a field of wilting poppies
let's stay .

. still not happy it's an act
nothing particular here where's circe at .

THRUM

If you're thrumming then you aren't listening.
You spent your school days
peering out of frosted windows
as opaque as the Red River.

If you didn't hear a word
then you were waiting for an energetic
thetic performance space
a thrill that could stun you awake.

Daydreamers are homely
homophones multiply in your grey matter
you are that writer in every window
in every classroom.

Bedsitting, you just might be the hinge
that you are, insolent in silence
headthrumming subjunctive word thrum
clear as sin.

MINE

It's all mine –
the endless substantia, the terse
lyric, the dream that cringes
awake at daybreak.

It's all mine –
the glacial neurosis
the shattered windows
the dour spectres
the translucent words.

It's all mine and I gave it pills
after I offered my stories and verse to the
student therapist in the claustrophobic clinic
after suicide versing and wintering on black ice.

It's all mine –
the notions of you
coated in notions
of pathophysiology.

I let you in to the
bitter thrush of home
the static psychic winter
but please note –
it's all mine.

DRIP

It's an intravenous drip that punctuates your position
most efficiently – an endless auditory ellipsis.
You are levelled on a stretcher, the fluorescent
light pelts your gaunt face.

You are up for the uptaking, rising for uprising.

The hallways are filled with reluctant
martyrs wincing for the camera.

The bag sags and sways in rhythm; the lights
hum off key, serenading you:

where have you been, what have you done
sad child in your tattered hospital gown
come down.

The intravenous drip is somewhat
constant until you need another bag.
You fall into dreams of splitting open
crystallized on the stretcher; the night
is saline.

SUGARBLOOD

The television is dream-tinged in the pastel
waiting room always.

My condition is terribly conditioned –
it happens and doesn't.

Sugarblood can't stop me.
Glitches happen – it's terrible.

Irradiated home informs specific
readings of illness; eyes roll endlessly.

We're mirrored in the translucent
skin, the oxygen tank, the syringe.

There's terror in the saline, terror
in the samples, saccharine trembling.

I am leaving slowly: health slippage.
Stay with me.

We could tremble to sleep under a
soft television flicker in a typical waiting room.

SAYINGS

What do I say to it?

Promising me flowers, promising me structure
stretched across the luminous classroom
it is flowering promises.

Saying conjures up tragic semantics
indolence in the lexicon.
It trips you up and me.

Say something darker.

THIS POEM IS ANDY KAUFMAN

This poem is Andy Kaufman.
It cowers and seethes in the digitized canon.
It plays with your cultural doctrine;
it makes strange with the sugar landlord.
It delves down under the bathroom sink;
it snarls at your knickers.
It sings off-key to an empty office;
it loves you.

Here is the emblematic structure of this poem:

A phonograph plays in an empty room with candy-red walls.
A cathartic needle feebly scrapes at your neck while you fake sleep.
The car you are driving is a grey 1981 Chevette with a racing stripe.
The dashing psychic surgeon asks you to light his clove cigarette.

Oh, and the phonograph is playing 'Love Me Tender'
and the needle is dirty
and the car is stolen
and the cigarette has a rich, smooth taste.

Dear Andy,

I wrote the first draft today. I think it works. It is as much a response to a challenge I presented myself in an earlier poem as it is a tribute to you or an invocation of you. When I think of you, which is far too often, I think of candy. I think I might try to write the poem again. I don't believe it's fair to cast you in such a saccharine mold. What happened to my words, Andy? I used to be so confident in them. You know the confidence of which I speak – that emulative confidence that permits one to play the villain, to swagger along the precipice. Anyway, I'm rambling. I don't want to trap you in mid-performance. This is really about me.

Your fiend,
JPF

This poem is Andy Kaufman.
It provides you with a suite.
It does not lack for friends;
it does not know this.
It does not know your number;
it wants your number.

It offers you gripe water;
it croons at your ankles.
It asks you for some patience
some semblance of cultural knowledge.
It asks you for the time;
it doesn't understand the twenty-four-hour clock.

It hates you;
it hates anything like you.
It wants you;
it wants anything like you.
It lets you sleep;
it lets you dream.

Here's the way this poem goes:

There's a videotape rewinding in an empty room;
the room is saccharine-red.
There's a vintage cartoon that you can't turn off;
you are half-disappointed.
There are professional possibilities going by in elliptical orbits;
you track them lethargically.

Dear Andy,

I am less pleased with my second draft than I was with my first. What kind of edit would you prescribe? I have been on the vial far too long. Outside my window drunken children scream obscenities. I've been drinking too. I've been drinking to you. What would your shtick have been if you had experienced the luxury of Effexor? You had Valium, right? That's something. Was Bob good to you? Was Lorne good to you? Was George good to you? Which one was Daddy? What the fuck? I promise to try again with a brand new poem. This one will lack the musicality of the former two but it will capture my relationship with you, which, despite my efforts, remains strikingly one-sided.

Your freud,
JPF

This poem is Andy Kaufman.
It loathes your attention span, your complicity.
It wrestles with gender;
its theory is forgettable, essential, essentialist.
It won't stop droning on;
it doesn't want to be onstage.
It wears sequins on its sleeve;
it forgets to pay the rent.

Here's what the poem attempts:

a UHF version of the town idiot
a broadcast appeal unfolding retroactively
a perfect flat save for minor water damage
a sharp haunting dulled by snowy reception.

But here's what you see:

It's 1977 and I am two years old; my older brother shuffles his feet across the thick orange shag and shocks me; you are on the television, crooning amid candied white noise; everything's red when I close my eyes no matter how dark it gets, no matter what I try; I spend the whole year trying.

Oh, and the poem is cunning
and the poem will shoplift
and the poem has issues
and to these, returns.

Dear Andy,

I'm sorry. I failed. I think you would have been proud. It turns out I won't be moving to Long Island after all. It turns out I was never planning to. What happened at Saddle Rock? Promise you'll tell me one day? Great Neck is burning down. I really must go. I will never write another poem. I will write only this one. One day, it will be on television.

Your fraud,
JPF

LET'S BURN DOWN WESTMOUNT

We can use the full night, turn a tinge
of subversive speech into action because
we can feel these walls keeping us out.
These walls do not fall.

Well ...

possibilities swell like your parents'
unaccounted-for bank accounts.

Let's burn down Westmount
take pills, insulate insular
take this city in a stretcher built for two
delve down to the pristine lawns
and make what is comfortable burn.

This is resistance.
Let's incite insight
ignite that ether
and let it stretch across the estates, the rented rooms.
Here is a paratactic night; the night is young.
Here is a universe – insurgent and subordinate.

Tonight, we will wake
under an insatiable sky
move toward the neighbourhood
hurl ourselves against a chain-link wall or two
hand in glove, pen in hand, pen to tongue, tongue in cheek.

LET'S BURN DOWN THE AUTHOR

The dreams and scrawls of
excitable speech – the wounds
creak open on every page
like extended-release pills.

We will have a wonderful time
enlightening the dead man
sparking up the world
letting the author's ember
flicker us to sleep.

BEDDING

Winter came too soon enough
to decorate every futile intention
and every domestic convention
with a light
dusting.

There is no reason not to stay
since we are already here
and so are our dreams
of unfulfilled narratives
etched into the well-versed
bedding.

Let's go bedding because it's winter
and maybe if we write imaginary seasons
create a decorative psychosis that just
might work or even just may be then
what?

Let's go out bedding because it's winter
and the tears freeze immediately
and the only solace is sophistic
verse and/or
speech.

Let's go to bedding because it's winter
and I'm feeling unsound and so tired
of embedding every desire in suspicious
words like unbedable or
misread.

SURGE. SCRAWL. STITCH.

scrawl on anonymous walls

the importance of thinking in idiom
the road to well is paved with
the sadness only lasts forever
dreaming you know the difference
if the streets are silent enough
you will dislocate the sentiment
you will provide the surge
you will will things to happen
with intricate stitching
you will lace your intention
it's all over – this cruel warmth
scrawl outside with permanent ink
let me read your etchings
let me in or let me sink
let me stitch you to me
dislocate me in a fleeting surge
it takes a great effort to fail
it's almost shocking
write me into difference
give me your voice
scrawl me with the most
electrical mixed metaphors
that unravel like

the contents of an adolescent bedroom

TRACKING

Finally living!

I am e-mailing myself a reminder.
I fear there is little hope for the recipient.

I'm spent. Reciprocity is mythic. Prosody is syphilitic.
Have you ever? Will you ever? Let me track you.

Haven't been keeping track. Oh Miserablism!
Rescue me and let me bring my diary.

White lies are wise. I have twenty-seven dollars
and my vintage tracksuit.

Tracks in the prairie snow: here's a regional tic.
Follow them to a fence; berate the demarcation.

I am writing one book ahead. I hope you get this.
I am about to click 'send.'

ALARMISTS

You can't get there from here.
You don't want to.

Oh, you can get there through letters.
You can get there through fiction.
Latinate letters: they create.

Oh, the metaflow
the lacquered, toxic diction
and drivel.

Alarmists in the garden
alarmists in the textbooks
insects in the intertext.

A rogue rewrites
a scholar inscribes.
It's all very pesticidal.

Alarmists in the canon
everyone squirming.

PACT UNPACKED

This is a pact between us:
we will end it all

if we find ourselves plastered with the look
of corporate faces – effortless, tacit, beaming

if we find ourselves escaping specificity in general
specifically waxing and waning off the clock

if we find ourselves in domestic body bags
twitching, sighing *help*

if our eyes are permanently rolled over this flat landscape
our dreams skyscraping themselves

if hours become silent ethereal hymns
perversely melodic and slow

if we feel too young
in the atoms we are ordered to breathe

if there are too many young people
erotically strewn across the right

if it's Sunday and everyone else has already done it
in a manner of speaking

if it's Saturday and we just can't
wait for Sunday

if we can do it at the exact same moment
in fantastic synchronicity

if we catch hold of some subatomic reality
and it makes sense

if it pleases us not to hurt anyone anymore
and so we don't

if I – sucking on an ashtray –
turn to you and utter melancholic, teenaged lyrics –

it is fatalistic and static
under the jaundiced stars tonight
and still I wish to know eternity
as sadistic as I expect it to be
come, let's repress in collectivity
let's decorate our illnesses
let's let go from any or every balcony
taste that novel air, land on the broken glass
of home, or let's find the perfect alley
to get trampled in

oh, how we would gurgle and smile
with every blow, receive the hate
with interpellated wisdom, reading
every bruise and gash symbolically
and we could squirm in our own
poetic realm of ash and tar and
oh, the possibilities, sensory and
imagistic.

DIME BAGS

The muses scatter their empty dime bags
and out of the seething earth
grey monoliths sprout and stretch.

They are stems made up of lazy friction
elevated botany and elevator veins
office-filled, reaching for the south.

Self-contained in the antiseptic sunlight
they are gleaming like unopened, gilded books.
Tourists mistake the colour for silver.

TONIC

Seven o'clock,
Miltonic time and
I'm writing this to tell
you not to bother to set
the alarm to wake me. I can't
perform any trace of heroism.
I can't pull down any pillars. Ruling
classes revise their dreams in the following
way – silkscreened on tasteless vellum, instantly
canonized and draped over the Philistines. I haven't
slept yet but the pillars are crumbling and while they
come down on their own, you are immersed in sitcom
theory, constructing elaborate pathetic fallacy in order
to capture tinned laughter. The walls are watching you
emote; they are creeping closer. I clamp my index finger
between my front teeth, roll my eyes. What if there never
were pillars to begin with?

What time is it?

ANTENNAE

Mother,

My trip was money well spent:
my dry spell meant the muse was bingeing.

Due to excessive governmental
bedpost notches, this will be
the last dispatch from the
gilded office:

Mother, the Tories suck, the Grits
suck and so do the suburbs;
I have nothing beyond this.
But wait, here's something:

a dream in which Father
shrouds the antenna in tinfoil
you are wrapped up in police tape
and I am almost happy.

LYSOL

We could be suffragists, disinfecting the deified sky
imploding cultural imperatives, ourselves.

We could rewrite things, etch them into our desks; maybe
phone me one day soon if you want to.

We could get high; this place has always been like an
invalid hymn; I don't love it – I came here to remember that.

We could hide under the pews. Do you want to?
I shoplifted some Lysol. Do you want some?

We could do it here; the choir always scares me
but nobody will hear a thing over their voices.

We could fall asleep.
We should fall asleep.

STRATEGIES FOR PATRONAGE

The means by which we can mean it –
something to do with seamless easywords.

Think of the wordroot patron in all of us;
give me a moment or two – I mean it.

We speak in performatives; this is the
only thing I know (I give it to you).

Meandrip in the throat, what have you
been up to, you insomniac?

Don't forget your sapphic ethic –
the means by which it will matter.

Later on when the sense returns, scratch
an ode to your dreamtrips.

Request honorariums for your
emotives; initial beside the commerce verse.

Outside a patron waits in line, disgendered
by layers of plain clothing, singing painsongs.

PERFORMATIVITY

Consider the following utterance:

'I'm leaving you.'

A statement that is performative in nature but not a primary performative, since it is hinged on the verb 'to be,' nor is it a true descriptive. What is really being said is the following: 'I + leave + you.' The verb 'to be' and its corresponding present participle are necessary evils, if you will. This could be considered a contractual, or perhaps counter-contractual, performative. But most importantly, this statement is an example that can be transgressive of the very nature of performativity if the following potentialities occur:

J1
If the speaking subject does not perform the act of leaving, if, in fact, the speaking subject does not intend to make any gesture of leaving other than the auditory performative, then the utterance can be filed under the category of an infelicity that operates on a principle of misinvocation. In this hypothetical instance, there is a hitch in the conduct. A true performative requires implied sincerity.

J2
If the speaking subject is not in the position to leave the addressee (there was never a relationship), or there is no addressee, then the category of infelicity is the misapplication. The presupposition of relational validity is the culprit.

J3
Hey! Listen, Mom. It's my walkman, not yours, and I'll be damned if I'm gonna let you lend it to your scab boyfriend. So you breastfed me for twelve glorious years. That doesn't mean you're really my mother. Why don't you take that fancy electric blue toaster of yours and light your own cigarette for a change? And for fuck's sake, get to work! That school bus ain't gonna drive itself. And what kind of a name is Karl anyway?

THE VERBIAGE BETWEEN US

the last time we talked about carrying on and you carried on about the fear of carrying on and how you were better off without I carried you home in my mind over the threshold thrush my mouth cracking and we held fast to the belief that the secrets we secreted were sacred I silenced you against the backdrop of silence the slings and narrow misses of juvenilia singing slinging my name in your voice you sucked on a coffee and I watched you watching me studying the faces of students failing to be studious moving in social ellipses is this unclear I asked you clearly you didn't mean to imagine I meant it then and I mean it now only I forget the subject matter of my assertion believe you me you may not whisper in concrete terms but I still know you and the tactics you employ moving toward tact or tract every word you said I feel is to be continued without feeling this idiosyncratic static you said I feel for you and I have a feeling that was your first best mistake imagine fleeing from my feelings you didn't claim this or that claim too busy fleecing me out of my mind you claimed last time as a prophecy of a larger discourse to come when one day comes one day I will understand the manifestation I will put the man back in manifestation in back in infestation you silenced me with the very notion of me in silence imagine it's a good thing I have a thick skin thick skin is thin blood is domestic don't dream if you had any sense you would have sensed it by now yet another coffee under the gentle illumination of fluorescent flesh don't imagine crawling out of this too much sense outside

NAMEDROP

You are in need of a namedrop straight off the fourteenth floor
reading each storey on your way down, dull lamplight, television
flicker and then right into traffic breaking your back,

or perhaps off a bridge as if you were in a filmic climax
headlong into undertow like a discarded tourniquet or a useless
leaking pen that used to lead to bliss.

At home, in your desk, the bliss is receding into
something more comfortable.
You are suddenly older, occupying cold skin.

You are not afraid of a namedrop now and then, a little Sylvia
never hurt anyone: tulips, skulls, imaginary red
hair, black yew tree, every building hospital-blue.

You are profound in the intravenous afternoon, with a
sketch pad and a case of lead poisoning, your name in
faint ink on your hospital wristband.

See the lady of Shalott down from her tower
sprawled out in her craft, piss- and punch-drunk
gurgling on the water?

You want to drop right there
but you are stitched to that bridge
just watching her, just weaving verse.

DARK STAR TEXT

Without words it gets colder and when the dark star rises late
I'm comfortably sedated so it feels right to blame you
for my wordlessness.

Without terms I am tacit and I blame you and the dark star
lingers, the teleprompter sputters, lags and it feels
half-right.

A flowering capital idea illuminates the antiseptic sky
the thick dark drip we are under; a bright retail malady
sweeps over a nation or two and lulls us to neversleep.

Ignore the television's blue virginal hiss and let's
dress unsuccessed and speak without words in tongues
just above or beneath breath.

The dark star sets.
Words germinate on
the translucent bedsheets of home.

Phone up your dark star.
Tell him that you love her.
Prove it.

Musing is dead.
Perhaps you should die too.
The girls have amnesia nightly.
The boys are working on vocations
in an unmarked night school.

So go to school with the girls and the boys
and peer through filthy
windows; fall asleep on your
favourite subject.

Trips into normalcy
reveal
the trance before
the words before
the dark star trance
the television sings
the phone hisses.

Instant-message your dark star.

ACQUIESCE

What is acquiescent is staged.

Parents, love your children as though they are visionary tracts.
Revise and resist formation of any static signifier
and adhere to whatever grammar you must.
Take them to the public with fervour.

Aggrandize the moment; mother the fetish.
Scrawl a mirror stage all over a pharmacy postcard and fail to acquiesce.

WILLING. WAITING.

I think of us without the drugs and it scares me.

We have been draped
in lucent schemes.

We have been swept into
pharmacy vials.

I'm willing to wait until I don't feel a thing.

I'm waiting to will the drugs to stop working.

I think of you as a kinder withdrawal.

We are spineless yet facing it.

And one day we just might
not wake up like we used
to.

Go ahead.
Scare me.

TREPANNING FOR DOLLARS

I wish I were bored. This isn't your poem. This isn't your problem. It's my decision and it's time for some bloodletting. Hold this drill bit. I might need it if the skull is stubborn. Voices need a way in. Genius needs an open-door policy. I need this. There is a flow to be achieved. I admit it won't be easy. There might be leakage. But ideas will spring forth and I need to write that book. Confirmation comes to those who will it. There will be no buyer's remorse. I need this. I need to breathe. Hand me that last spike. This is about ideological ventilation. When I'm properly punctured I will sing like a haloed crooner. Right now I'm almost tapped, dreaming of cranial dilation. This is a kinder, gentler catechism. I am moving beyond – into the post-Tylenol era. Where's my pickaxe? Where's my conscience? Where's my head at? I need to be bored.

IT'S JUST THAT

It's not that I'm holding on so much
as I'm holding my breath,
turning to you shamefully cold and easy
on the strictest, loveliest summer day.

It's not that lovely a day.
It's strict in its presentation:
there's a filthy nunnery;
there's a strip mall with gleaming windows;
there's an inversion in the air.

It's not that last-ditch grasp tongue lashing.
The world loves you just the way you aren't.
Stay grasping.

It's not that I don't see past your thinly veiled traipse
your traipsing verve
your verse impositions.

It's just that.

It's just that today is the only day you've ever known.

It's just that it feels better when someone is strict.
There's a list of suitable tropes you would rather
not get into right now.

It's just that it's better this way.
Just let me have it:
inversions pockmark the sky you wish you were
grasping, holding, so much, so strict, so lovely.

STREP SONG

You are singing

at the monolithic gate of the
university

in the gleaming parkade with a pocketful
of pills

on the seminary steps with a throat
full of strep.

The air is full of winter and it's
May Day in the silent, psychic city.
The air is full of winter and it's
May Day in the silent, psychic city.

You are singing

singing strepped on the steps, on the lawn, in the car
singeing the city in and out of 3/4 time within the
seductive difficulty of song, disseminating.

meant to in numbers because of the power there is into menthol breath and hover again because it never ends, this thread of verse, the old ones only sever their knowledge, love of it – don't forget to get wrapped up in emotionality while you wait not yet the rapt reader dives in novelistic leave the breed behind everything must get dyed

meant to in lessons because of the power there is in pedagogy, just ask the lesser ones, the Poundian verve of knowing you think you are right and frightening rush of vowing to keep to yourself the fact that you can't get caught, let go of the conviction it can't do anyone any harm any more than you can

do on your own with a pen and some emulated charm, here come the years of *I meant to* with ribboning songs thrummed to tears and the drift departs now, farewell to the normals the game shows, and farewell to the pleasure vehicles, the dreary, hello to the old ones, the fellows who enrapture the ageist dream, and hello serotonin

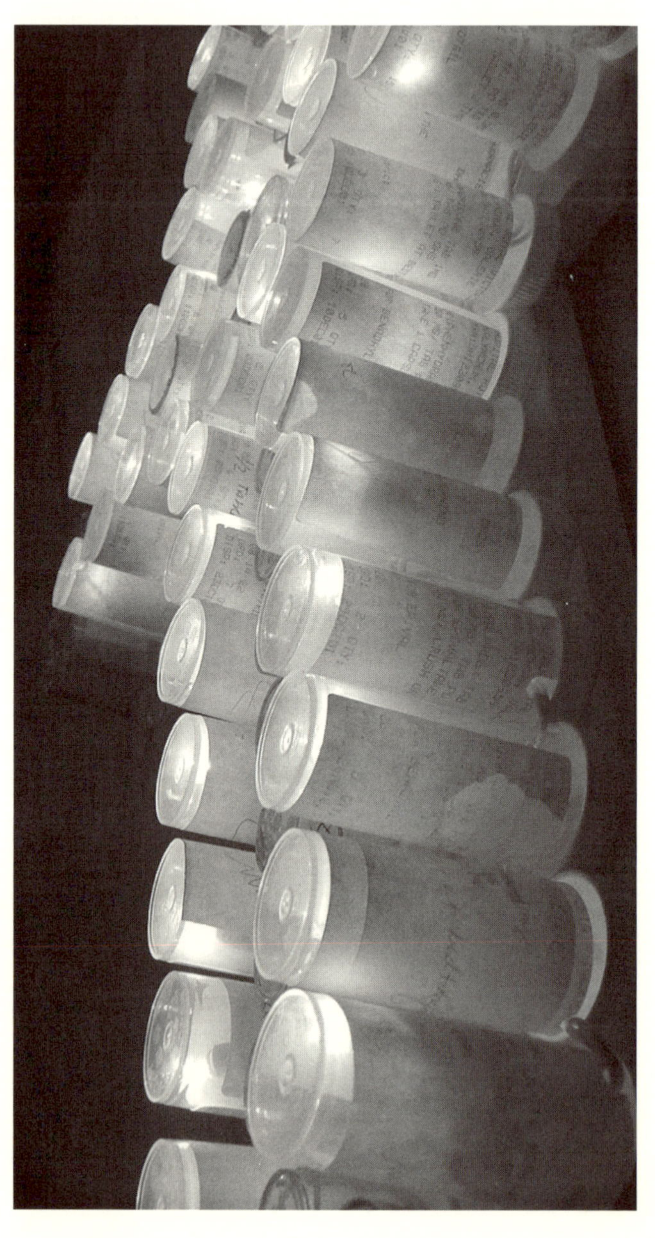

HOMECALLINGS

ANCHORAGE

You are a victim of anchorage.
You create it.

The idea is tethered –
the disenchanted home leash.

Stop anchoring to bungalows.
Stop anachronistic breath.

Leave pleasantland.
Leave the shingled sonnet.

Please the victim anchor.
Please leave.

THE SWITCHING YARD SONG

Here, the sky sickens its way into your sleep;
it whimpers in your ear, drips on your
tongue, so endless and pointless.

It's a prairie sky after all, with a pristine
meaning.

Living in flatland is neologistic; at times it
strains sense, stains pallid skin, permits tense
tenement dreams to spread, germinate on an
ice-laced plain; and the sky here still persists.

And I'm here now, home now, with medicinal
verve, with blistering ink on pharmacy receipts.
The words drift eastward and are hooked back
into the intermodal, like an AM broadcast.

But the overwrought, overcast sky
is larger than sin.

It is not recalling but retelling
home.

Thin wisps of pollen and dandelion seeds swathe flatland.
Highbeams drape over the mythic switching yard.

The switching yard is glimpsed in drips.

The sky disjunctively pricks out its meaning.

+ + +

The switching yard lures you to sleep with minor strains:

its blasphemous untouchable rusting lush

its hypoallergenic hyperallegorical luminous transit

its somnambulant treacherous soma

its adjectival narcoleptic mourning.

The switching yard takes you to all of this
and if you lived here you might even concede
that it's almost lovely.

+ + +

Winnipeg derailed years ago
still, twisted, rotting, fucked up
under a clay sky.

Just take two
milligrams
in the morning
like I do.

    Oh my screeching iron lung . . .

Sparks jump off the rails.
Asbestos disperses through retail.

I am leaning into rails in the east.

You are railing against the curse where you are.

+ + +

Strike me all the way to last call.
Strike me like I'm family.
Strike me in parenthetical disjunction.
Strike me (don't strike me).
Strike me hypermelodically.
Strike me until the switching yard sings us to sleep.

DEEP WINTER

beat on the brat, beat on the brat
beat on the brat with a baseball bat
– Joey Ramone

Hit me so hard I fell off your handlebar
got trapped in your spokes
was dragged through the icy street.

I was yours
eyes widened before the swelling.

I stood in the middle of the playground
in the middle of my development.

I stencilled myself to the side of
Arthur Day Junior High School again.

I slept in your garden that night
listened to your parents whisper.

I was sleeping and not dreaming at all
awakened by allergy.

Adulthood seeped in
absorbing imagination and breath.

Don't leave me;
console me with hatespeech.

Lay me down in the storage freezer
in your unheated basement
in deep winter.

MISSION STREET SONG

Take an eight-cylinder engine
down to Mission Street.
Race the trains
and lose every time.

Take seven Gravol tablets
and wake up to ironic cricketsong
and the West Nile
in your blood.

Place your work on your tongue
and swallow slowly.
Sprawl out on prairie tall grass;
preserve it with your nostalgic lapses.

Settle in St. Boniface;
photocopy your lexicon.
Send it Priority Post
to the National Library.

Wake up again to Winnipeg
on Mission Street.
Listen to the song
of the grey city:

> your entire family
> the police officers
> the trains
> the teenaged cars
> the social workers
> the safe houses
> the scrapyards
> the playgrounds
> are crooning 'disrepair.'

DAUPHIN 1981

Deciphering

Gary Carter or Tim Wallach
sprint through television snow
my great-grandfather pissing
on my bedroom door at two in the morning

costume jewellery and fresh snow shimmer
five long minutes without being watched
too much family condensed into unopened chests
jaundiced paper and a jaundiced kitchen

preserves.

TRANSCONA 1986

Curled up on yellow shag carpet
or weak-ankled in
plastic micron skates.
I am twelve.
My lungs are fifty.

Oxford Heights Community Club
where they drive me to cower –
Saturday afternoon for practice
Sunday night for games.

In winter, the prairie air steals your
breath then suspends it in mid-air.

I have a blue inhaler.
I have a beige inhaler.

TRANSCONA LOL

I know Transcona.

I have seen the wintering children
choking on tinsel.

I have served the ten-year-old mother
thrift shopping for LSD.

I have delved into that
solvent-drenched solvency.

I have slept in creaking single beds
etched with lyric dreams.

I have lingered in frigid back lanes
with the Winnipeg artists
searching for youth and youths to use.

I have inhaled that spirit
the worker statuesque against
a harsh prairie wind.

I have been knocked out
under your catalytic converter.

Sometimes we meet in low-lit chat rooms
and you pine for those moments of epiphany.
Mescaline at the sand pits, you don't know what
you're missing.

I know your childhood:

drenched in motor oil and covered with stolen cigarettes
your corrupt paper routes, your retail scams
your lectures on shoplifting, your uncomfortable bedroom
your discomforting rhetoric.

Your cursor blinks lethargically. Hanging on
to consciousness, you type: remember that
night we got right pissed and broke into that
abandoned disco and we shattered all
the lights?

All these fucking tombstones
all these feeble structures

broken mechanics splitting open at the sports bar
broken high heels waiting in line at the LC
broken shopping carts on the driveways
broken televisions glistening on sidewalks

a landscape of hatchbacks rolling through stop signs.

I know Transcona.

You don't know what you're misreading.

In the chat room you listen to breath
the sun is threatening to rise and your
nostalgia level remains frighteningly high.
On graduation night we took the spray paint
to the school, as if we had anything to
communicate with such fleeting permanence.

I know why I can't go back.

I have rested in the rusting cars
the ones in which you would
promise yourself to someone
new every weekend.

The family is broken now
laid off and waylaid
down at the Central Hotel
sipping their way to sleep.

You are swallowed by your cursor
ultimately reducible, stuck in a loop
of reductive speech: LOL.

I know where to find Transcona:

somewhere between
the rusting train yards
and the peeling fences.

I suppose I'm coming back.
Meet me behind the old folks' home.
I'll bring the spirits if you bring the solvents.
If you bring the permanent marker

I'll bring the words.

HOMECALLING

always
home calling

power lines tighten and
sag in and out of season

block heaters click
'plug her in if you want her to run'
think about that idiom

lips stuck to pole tongue stuck to tongue

'she was always a good little car'

pine for a self-serve self
it's winter at home
we have antifreeze in the blood
a make-believe city in the middle

always in the middle of something
and never enough time to call

polemics of dialing
listen in to home
always in the meddling

listen:
not home

HAZEL DELL

The streets were lined with Dutch elm disease –
regal trees with weeping branches and neon orange
spray-painted trunks.

The air was perfumed with thistle breath and the Red River.
Crabgrass seeped through chain-link; every
driveway was crooked.

She ran over the three-year-old child with her
wood-panelled minivan; she said it felt just like
a speed bump.

The Red River's undertow was always present
in every alcove and every makeshift, splintered
playground
pulling.

TRAPPING

Wanderlust is tragic. Canada hasn't germinated long
enough to trap it.

Formalists lose interest in lists; they prefer long-winded tropes to
sayings that thrum.

Forsake the hyperpostal world. Trip, drunk on a halogen
livingroom DVD mantra.

Traipse the rotting mall. Make a manic
installment payment.

There's a long history of trapping here. I come from a long line
of trapped people – mall walkers.

The Arctic is where they place me, placate me.
Paterson NJ is where I wanted, wasn't wasted.
Transcona MB is a mythic howl, scripted bitch, bitter tripe.

PRAIRIELIT

Piles of hometrips.
Strips of mallkids.
Dreams of sleeptext.
Miles of phonesleet.
Steads of fencedhope.
Drips of graindrain.
Sheets of inkstrain.
Streets of wheatlash.
Sinks of draindrought.
Drafts of litwaste.
Fits of lispdraft.
Tastes of christdust.
Weeks of seedspite.
Maps of frostnode.
Wisps of glasstrips.
Trips of streetdrift.
Homes of angstsong.

ACKNOWLEDGEMENTS

Earlier versions of 'Psychometrics' and 'Dopamine Song' were published in *Transcona Fragments* (Winnipeg: Cyclops Press, 2002). 'Let's Burn Down Westmount,' 'Strategies For Patronage' and 'Neurotransmission' were published in *Stonestone*. 'Hello Serotonin' was published as an above/ground broadside: #141. 'Dark Star Text' and 'Surge. Scrawl. Stitch.' were published in *Evergreen: Six New Poets* (Windsor: Black Moss Press, 2002). 'Transcona 1986,' 'Dauphin 1981,' 'It's Just That,' and 'Homecalling' were published in *Contemporary Verse 2*. 'Pact Unpacked' was published in *nthposition*. 'Takeup 2' and 'Takeup 3' were published in *Eleven: A Tart Magazine Supplement*. 'prairielit' was published as an above/ground broadside: #161. 'Lysol,' 'Dime Bags,' 'Deep Winter,' 'Antennae,' 'Performativity' and 'Mission Street Song' were published in *Juice*'s Featured Writer section. 'Hazel Dell' and 'Mission Street Song' were published in *Maisonneuve*. 'Transcona 101' was published in *dANDelion*. The sound art version of 'Mission Street Song' was featured in the limited edition CD *Urban Slices* (*Juice* insert).

'Some Thoughts on Strict Cons' is for Jay MillAr.
'Namedrop' is for Sarah Steinberg.
'Pact Unpacked' is for Chandra Mayor.
'Mission Street Song' is for Clive Holden.

Thanks to Jay MillAr, Alana Wilcox, Jason McBride, Sarah Steinberg, David McGimpsey, Mary di Michele, Catherine Hunter, Robert Budde, Robert Allen, Chandra Mayor, Clive Holden, MC Palassio, Andy Brown, Valerie Joy Kalynchuk, Rick/Simon and my family.

Special thanks to Tara Flanagan.

ABOUT THE AUTHOR

Jon Paul Fiorentino is a Winnipeg/Montreal poet and editor. His previous poetry collections include *Resume Drowning* (Broken Jaw Press, 2002) and *Transcona Fragments* (Cyclops Press, 2002), which was a finalist for the 2002 Carol Shields Winnipeg Book Award. He is the editor of *Career Suicide!: Contemporary Literary Humour* (DC Books, 2003) and a contributing editor for *Matrix* magazine. Jon can be visited online at www.jonpaulfiorentino.com

Typeset in Scala and printed and bound at the Coach House
on bpNichol Lane, Toronto

Edited by Jay MillAr
Copy edited by Alana Wilcox
Cover by Rick/Simon
Cover visual art by Valerie Joy Kalynchuk and Jon Paul Fiorentino
Interior art by Valerie Joy Kalynchuk, from *Crux*
(installation, 2003), as photographed by Andy Brown
Author photo by Karen Paquin

Coach House Books
401 Huron Street (rear) on bpNichol Lane
Toronto, Ontario
M5S 2G5

1 800 367 6360

mail@chbooks.com
www.chbooks.com